Do Houses Dream?

Poems by
Barbara Novack

BLUE LIGHT PRESS

Finalist for the Blue Light Press 2015 Poetry Prize

Do Houses Dream?

BOOK & COVER DESIGN
Melanie Gendron

Author Photo:
S. Rita J. Vanson, CIJ

ISBN: 978-1-4218-3755-0

1ST WORLD LIBRARY
PO Box 2211
Fairfield, Iowa 52556
www.1stworldpublishing.com
Email: worldlibrary@lisco.com

BLUE LIGHT PRESS
www.bluelightpress.com
Email: bluelightpress@aol.com

To my parents
with love and gratitude

It takes a village . . .

Thank you

Kathy and Chris and Trisha and Bob
The Friday group: Fred, Julie, Elvira, Richie, and Lenny
My Oceanside Library family
My Rockville Centre Public Library family
Bruce
Debby
Joel

Table of Contents

Acknowledgments

These poems first appeared in the same or similar form in the following publications:

"Elsewhere" in *The Cape Rock*

"September" in *The Nassau Review*

"Flowers of Autumn" in *The Weekly Avocet* #98

"Sea and Sand, a Boardwalk and a Man" in Walt's Corner in *The Long Islander*

"White" Award winner, Nassau County Poet Laureate Society 2016 Poetry Contest; included in *Nassau County Poet Laureate Society Review*, Vol. IV

Elsewhere

A snippet of found film
only minutes long
fifty feet of the past
scattershot and skittish
spinning a long gone world
bouncing from bungalow to bungalow
treetop to treetop
sky to road to sky
until it settles
like a skipping stone
on a swimming pool
and splashing bathers
forty years ago:

Then the world was young.
The future is an elsewhere there.
I was two, in my father's arms,
he teaching me to swim
holding me
safe
as I splashed in the water
I giggling, he laughing
joy in his little girl.
He hands me to my mother,
the ever unswimmer happy in an inner tube,
and she props me against her
my legs out on the tube
and I am hugged, safe
and smiling.

I stretch one leg high
enjoying
where I am
who I am.

I do not remember
a world so young;
we were then
older than
we'd ever been.

All that
is elsewhere now
lost
but for these moments.
I watch
over and over
knowing what will come
not knowing what will be
wishing I could once again touch
what we were.

A Poem for My Father

The books were old, pages beige and crumbly
but the words were poetry
and you read them to me
with smiles and joy.

And you recited from eager memory
poems of Hiawatha and the ride of Paul Revere
and verses from Stevenson's child's garden.

And you always said your sisters
the aunts I knew who sent me birthday books
were prize-winning poets in high school.

I didn't always know I would write poetry
the way some say they do,
but because of you
poetry
pumped through my heart,
ran through my veins
and sang in me

long before
my words
reached the page.

Five Photographs

Twenty-seven pictures on the roll and
I'd shot twenty-two,
pictures I wanted to see
trips and sights and events,
important things;
five pictures unshot kept me
from developing the roll
now past its expiration date;
pictures have a blue tinge
developed past the expiration date.
I needed to finish off the roll.

It was a nice day and my father
was doing his usual thing outdoors
popping the hood of his car
peering inside
leaning over the mechanism
wiping, cleaning, testing, tinkering
and later, out in the backyard,
he would water his plants,
the tomatoes, green peppers,
cucumbers and zucchini
that rimmed the yard on two sides, and
his rose bushes and marigolds
on the third side.

I had five pictures to get through
on a roll of film
past its expiration date.

I took the camera outside
snapped two of him at his car
three of him watering his plants,
throwaways that would come out blue anyway.
He laughed; it all seemed silly to him
and a waste, not something to photograph, just
him doing ordinary things
on a summer afternoon.

Photographs of trips, sights and events pale.
In five photographs of the ordinary
that finished a roll of film
and are not blue at all,
my father lives.

September

The pear tree in the neighbor's backyard
drops its crop on the driveway
with hard thumps
like baseballs hitting a mitt.
But the pears roll, uncaught.

Once my father climbed to the top of the garage
where the pear tree branches stretch over the peak
and perched there, straddling it, plucking pears
and tossing them down to me. I
caught each neatly,
brown-green balls of sweetness, small and firm,
slapping into my cupped palms
and deposited in a large paper bag at my feet.
The pluck, the toss, the catch, the drop:
we had a good rhythm that sunny September afternoon.
And when the bag was finally full and the game ended,
my father lit his pipe, set it at a jaunty angle,
and sat secure and serene
up high against the bluest sky.

The pear tree in the neighbor's backyard
drops its crop on the driveway
with hard thumps:
the pears roll, uncaught.

I stand at the kitchen window
and stare out at the branches
so high against
the emptiest sky.

Unveiling: June 28, 1998

We stand before your draped stone
a year, a month and a day later
to unveil it,
to say prayers,
to touch again the soul that rose.
The stone is my design,
a personal tribute,
from the fire department Maltese cross
on the lower left
to the dove flying out of frame
on the upper right.
(There had to be that shield:
it was so much a part of you;
there had to be a bird,
so much a part of us,
backyard watchers from the kitchen window.
I bought you bird books to identify them
and found your handwritten note
between the pages.)
And the inscription,
your name, your dates, of course,
the necessary Hebrew I can't translate,
your sister's characterization —
A truly noble man —
ours, by way of Shakespeare —
We shall not see his like again —
so true, so true.

And we undrape the stone
to the nodding approval of the gathered,
and we say the required prayers
and I say my own, written
just for you:

The universe is energy,
life is energy.
Energy is never lost,
only changed. . . .

And though you are the dove flown
out of the frame,
I know you are
not lost
only changed.

Sea and Sand, a Boardwalk and a Man

A photograph of my father
on a boardwalk, beach and ocean to his right.
He wears slacks and a white shirt.
Wind whips his dark hair.
He is smiling, but
not quite at the camera.

I remember the moment,
him standing there, waiting for my mother
always slow with the click
to snap the photo.
I remember his gaze shifting
to me, five years old, at my mother's side.
I remember the smile,
not for the camera, not at all for the camera.
I remember smiling back at him.

The photograph is timeless,
nothing there to date it.
No cars, no women's fashions.
Just sea and sand, a boardwalk and a man
smiling at me
for eternity.

Cookies

My mother, after being sick for eight months,
found energy and
baked cookies Thursday night. Not
her usual ones from her mother's complicated recipe
but from a recipe in the newspaper,
"Easy Oatmeal Raisin Cookies in One Pot."
"It *looked* easy," she said
as one pot led to many
and measuring cups and spoons
and much to wash, and dough
that first clumped and burned
and then finally baked golden and chewy
and so tasty we can't stop eating them.
"Not many calories," she says, pleased with our response,
"all good ingredients,"
and she rattles them off — "oatmeal, eggs, milk, raisins"
— and qualifies —
"just a pinch of sugar, just a touch of oil."
Can't be fattening, we conclude,
wishing she'd baked more as
the level in the clear glass cookie jar
drops precipitously.

My mother, after being sick for eight months,
found energy and
baked cookies Thursday night
and life was briefly
as it should be.

The Power of Tears

Waking, half off the bed,
clutching the bedclothes to keep from falling:

Tears
wet the pillow,
tears
that do not dry.
They move the earth with quaking,
carve canyons in the soul,
drench the desert of the heart,
nourishing seeds to flower,
coloring the world with the painted bloom
of salt rain.

Half off the world, I
clutch the dream
to keep from falling.

What Matters (2014)

So much seems to matter,
the books, the clothes, the rooms' décor,
the laundry, the sweeping, the dusting
the mowing, the clipping, the planting and picking,
the plans, all that and more
seem to matter
and then
the books stand in piles, the clothes on their racks,
the rooms' paint and paper peel; the walls are cracked
the laundry, sweeping, dusting undone,
others mow and clip to maintain a façade, while
nothing is planted or picked, nothing new begun.

In the end, at the end
there is only
sleeping, waking
and the presence of those who love

and maybe that
is all
that matters.

White

The white world this winter is not snow
with its natural sun-borne brightness
but sheets and walls
and rubber-soled shoes.
Nurses used to wear starchy white uniforms.
Now all wear soft flowery scrub tops
and pastel pants
pretending to be hopeful spring
and they are not all nurses.
They are the servers and sweepers and wipers
but their shoes are still white.

And whiteness is like snow blindness
my eyes searing
from the too muchness of it.
I cannot see her so small against the sheets,
lost in this late-life storm.
I close my eyes to it
and see painted on my lids, so clear,
the smile
I miss.

Now, when I speak and speak and speak
and try to pierce the whiteout,
she sometimes returns
with pale glazed eyes, yet
they clear
as her hand touches mine.

I wait for her lips to move
corners turning up
for the warmth of her sunlight
to wash over
the white.

Empty

Empty
the space against the sky
where the pear tree once stood
empty
the space in my life
where my mother lived:

The early morning buzz
of the saw
awakened me;
the early morning ring
of the phone
awakened me.

After a year's reprieve
what is
is not yet reality
just emptiness
a void
where something once breathed
and sighed
and, lit with sunshine,
laughed.

Leaf by leaf, then branch by branch
pared down to the trunk
to its basic self
then piece by piece
till it's a nub
and it is done.

Bit by bit, breath by breath
wearied down
winding down,
bit by bit, breath by breath, death
stilled the hand
so recently covering mine
in comfort,
and that too is done.

Swiftly efficiently
within the waking hour
years of love
become firewood
and dust.

She can no longer sweetly reach:
our mother-daughter embrace is cold,
and the pears will no longer fall each September
ripe and heavy, unpicked to roll.

Yet,
memory is
a succulent fruit.
Memory is what I hold.

Fill In the Blanks

This summer was _____
It felt _____
I went _____

dark
dark
nowhere

Each day was _____
Each night was _____
The season was _____

dark
dark
nowhere

It was a void
filled with emptiness
space
unfilled with meaning.

It was gray
like a storm on the horizon,
thunder booming
lightning cracking
the whip of the season
lashing
but the rain
waited

waited
the sky charcoaling
thunder booming
lightning cracking
storm
waiting

a blank to be filled
with meaning
with storm-rage and rain
running in rivers
down the streets

like tears

with the sky charcoaling
thunder booming
lightning cracking
and the storm
waiting

holding its anger
for
(fill in the blank)
What is anger for anyway?
Raging at the dying of the light
doesn't slow the dying.

The storm waits

for its own time.

Not mine.

Life is a blank
to fill in,
a season
of being
sandwiched between before and after
more blanks to fill in
sometime
when the void
fills with meaning.

Flowers of Autumn

We think of flowers as a summer thing
maybe spring
for the daffodils and such, the early birds
whose brightness lights the
waning days of winter.
But it is autumn now,
days-old season, and
the garden mums, the
three-dollar bushes I bought
last year (when there was more life around us
though they didn't bloom and two of the four
didn't even survive),
those garden mums alongside the garage
in the bare lane that held my father's tomatoes
and has been fallow since
gardening ceased with him,
those garden mums in sight of
my mother's day lilies
that bloomed briefly this summer
as if in tribute to her passing,
those two bushes, full and lushly green
in July
budding in multitudinous expectation
in August
have burst forth
in sequence
in September
glowing with gold and russet light
glory for the season
and a candle
for the night.

Alone

Her clothes are in the closet,
in her drawer, lipstick and comb:
I think she's coming home.

I think she's coming home.
Her things are all around
shoes and coats
shampoo and soap
her pots and pans
and favorite foods
from brown rice to honey grahams,
yet nothing is the same.

Nothing is the same
Still I think she's coming home
I feel it in my bones . . .
because
I feel so alone.

I feel so alone.
How can I think it looks the same?
How can I think she's coming home?
When everything has changed . . .

and I am alone.

Do Houses Dream?

Do houses dream
throb with placeness peopled
once
peopled by not-ghost essences?
I smell their scents
the ice-cream-cone aroma'd smoke
      of his pipe
the yeasty, sugar-laden heat
      of her baking;
I hear her bedroom-destined footsteps
      on the second-floor stairs
I hear him rattling his tools
      in his basement workroom
and sometimes they speak
not the late-night
      whisperings
but whisperings still
of comfort, consolation
caring and concern.
Do houses dream
or merely hold them gently
recognizing the egg-shell fragility
of memory?

About the Author

Barbara Novack, Writer-in-Residence at Molloy College, is also a member of their English Department. She founded and hosts Poetry Events and Author Afternoons, two reading series at Molloy College that bring contemporary poets and writers to a wider audience, and she presents programs and conducts workshops on poetry, fiction, non-fiction and memoir in the New York metropolitan area. Recent books include *Something Like Life* (poetry) and *J.W. Valentine* (novel). An award-winning writer, she is listed in the *Directory of American Poets and Fiction Writers* and *Who's Who of American Women*. Her website is www. barbaranovack.com.

www.ingramcontent.com/pod-product-compliance
Lightning Source LLC
Chambersburg PA
CBHW021917040426
42447CB00007B/906